Becoming a Compelling Communicator for Conservation

The Essential Reference for Everyone Who Desires to Make a Difference

William C. Dunn PhD

ISBN: 1494885832
ISBN 13: 9781494885830

To Dad,
who taught me that words are most power-
ful when the fewest possible are used.

The message is clear: eschew obfuscation!
—Dr. W. Leslie Pengelly

Acknowledgments

Bruce Milne, my good friend and doctoral advisor from the University of New Mexico (UNM) Department of Biology, assisted with the original manuscript, which was written for upper division ecology and sustainability studies courses. Valerie Thomas, UNM Department of English, provided helpful comments that improved the chapter on writing. Also providing helpful comments on earlier drafts of this book were Colleen Caldwell, leader of the US Geological Survey's Wildlife Research Unit, New Mexico State University; Kerry Murphy, wildlife biologist for Bridger-Teton National Forest; Sue Consolo-Murphy, Chief of Resources for Grand Teton National Park; and Guy Miller, US Forest Service (retired). Sarah Reynolds designed the front cover. Most of all, I am indebted to my wife, Katie, who hung in there with me on this project even when she thought I might be wiser to use the time to solicit more contracts for my consulting business.

Foreword

Effective communication is critical to getting conservation done. The best conceived and executed studies only make a difference when they convince their audience of the value of the data and the proposed actions. And audiences will only be convinced of that value if they understand the study and what difference it can make. After all, as a conservationist, making a difference with your results is the whole point of your work, right?

If you have been in the conservation business awhile, you no doubt have read many, many studies and watched a wide array of presentations. It's no accident you tend to remember the really bad and really good ones. The difference is that you generally remember *how* the bad ones were written or presented but *what* the good ones said. Those who present science and conservation well use a common set of tools. Providing those tools is what this book is about.

Whether it's the tweets and hashtags of the social media or the ever-increasing number of ecological and conservation journals full of new studies, competition for the attention of peers and decision makers is becoming increasingly acute. Thus, the need for an attention-grabbing message is ever more important. However, grabbing the attention of your audience, whether through writing or speaking, should not require sacrificing substance. This book shows you how to keep the science solid even while you ensure that the context of the message is clear and compelling.

I began collaborating with Bill in 1999 on a project for the New Mexico Department of Game and Fish in which we investigated innovative ways to map and manage big game hunts. During that project, Bill showed me how one can communicate with attention to detail, humble humor, and the requisite passion for conservation. I'm still inspired by Bill's memorable oral presentations because he consistently gave them his best, no matter who the audience was.

The tools that he used to effectively communicate throughout his career are now available in this text. Just as Strunk & White's *The Elements of Style* has been a ubiquitous reference of professionals, so this book should be on every conservationist's desk or loaded on his or her tablet. It is an invaluable guide. Simply put, I wish this book had been written years earlier. My career—and my audiences—would have benefitted from it.

Kurt Menke, GISP
Bird's Eye View GIS

Table of Contents

Chapter 1. Introduction

Most conservation happens only if the public supports it. Too bad the public doesn't care. At least that is what some data lead us to believe. When asked in a 2013 poll which issues were "very important," twice as many respondents chose the economy (75%) over the environment (37%). Health care (70%) and job creation (69%) ranked second and third; the environment ranked fourteenth of fifteen issues.[1] These same priorities were reflected in federal spending. For fiscal year 2013, the combined budget of all conservation and environmental agencies was 3.4% of the Department of Health and Human Services budget, 3.6% of the Social Security Administration budget, and 5% of the Department of Defense budget.[2]

Anyone passionate about conservation and the environment, like I am, will find these figures more than a bit discouraging. But before we throw in the towel, consider the following: in annual polls from 2000 to 2013 that focused only on environmental issues,[3] a solid majority of respondents on average chose "fair deal" or "great deal" to describe their worry about the environment (71%), concern about extinction (64%), and concern about habitat loss (82%). Additionally, 61% were either active in, or sympathetic toward, environmental matters.

1 www.rasmussenreports.com/public_content/archive/mood_of_america_archive/ importance_of_issues/economy_health_care_continue_to_lead_list_of_important_issues

2 www.whitehouse.gov/sites/default/files/omb/budget/fy2013/assets/budget.pdf

3 www.gallup.com/poll/1615/environment.aspx

Together, these seemingly disparate datasets yield an interesting message. Conserving nature and the environment does concern Americans, but that concern is easily overshadowed by other issues, particularly finances and health. So the take-home message seems to be this: public support for conservation is available, but it will not be handed to conservation professionals on a silver platter. The public has to be convinced of its value. Doing so requires rigorous science, sound management—and communication that commands respect and attention.

In 2003, Dr. David R. Anderson of the US Geological Survey and his colleagues published an excellent paper in the *Wildlife Society Bulletin* in which they called for improved scientific rigor in the wildlife profession[4]. A year later, I published a response in the same journal in which I added "improved communication skills" to their list of needs[5]. I had good reasons for suggesting this. College curricula for natural resource majors are heavily weighted toward teaching natural history, ecological principles, and quantitative methods—and rightfully so. After all, mastery of these subject matters is foundational to becoming a skilled professional. Unfortunately, learning how to share that knowledge with internal (peers and coworkers) and external publics usually takes a back seat. Formal training in communication all too often is limited to basic courses in English composition and public speaking with ad hoc practical application offered through term papers and oral presentations in core courses. Some students readily capture proper communication techniques; others do not. The result is a wide variation in capabilities among conservation professionals.

Resources to improve communication skills are not in short supply. These include books and videos with general lessons on public

---

4 Anderson, D. R., E. G. Cooch, R. J. Gutierrez, C. J. Krebs, M. S. Lindberg, K. H. Pollock, C. A. Ribic, and T. M. Shenk. 2003. Rigorous science: suggestions on how to raise the bar. Wildlife Society Bulletin 31:296-305.

5 Dunn, W. C. 2004. In my opinion: more suggestions on raising the bar for conservation——a response to Anderson et al. Wildlife Society Bulletin 32:594-597.

speaking, books or book chapters on how to write scientific articles or present research at professional conferences, and author guidelines for professional journals. The problem is that some of these resources are difficult to find, few address all the major components of communication used in conservation, and many provide more detail than a busy professional has time to digest.

Thus I designed this book not as an exhaustive treatise but as a concise compilation of the essential lessons of communication in conservation. For the student, it is a tutorial of what needs to be mastered before entering the profession. For the conservation professional, it is a refresher of knowledge that may have gotten buried under the pile of everyday responsibilities.

I chose the contents of this book based on what I learned during thirty-plus years as a professional wildlife and landscape ecologist, including sixteen with the New Mexico Department of Game and Fish. During those years, I developed writing skills by publishing and reviewing professional journal articles, writing and directing development of species management plans, preparing contracts and supervising the resulting scientific research, and preparing briefing papers for senior managers. I developed speaking skills through presentations to the New Mexico State Game Commission and a wide variety of scientific and public audiences. I also have been a keen observer of the presentations of others.

This book consists of four chapters of lessons of which three—chapters two through four—focus mostly on how to communicate to an audience. However, communication is a two-way street, and what you learn from others may be more important than anything you tell them. Indeed, it can be essential for earning that support that the public does not hand to us on a silver platter. In Chapter 5, I focus on two situations where receiving input is a priority—namely meetings with decision makers and with interested publics. If done right, these meetings can greatly enhance your ability to accomplish conservation.

Chapter 2. Laying the Foundation

Success in communication requires being well organized. Determining a clear direction, identifying critical components to include, and identifying pitfalls to avoid will make the journey to a compelling message more enjoyable and the challenges along the way more solvable. If you are embarking on original research, the four steps of planning discussed below should be completed well before you begin your study to ensure that you correctly sample, analyze, and interpret data. How you communicate will be of little consequence if what you communicate is flawed.

The planning process should lay a foundation so your message is **clear**, **concise**, and **complete**. I call these traits my **three C's** of communication and they form the basis for every lesson in this book. As discussed in the introduction, conservation and environmental issues face stiff competition for the attention of the public. Because of this, conservation professionals almost always are faced with a limited window of opportunity to make their case. Thus, it is imperative to be well prepared and to get to the point. If nothing else, your audience will appreciate that you value their time.

Brainstorm

Identify your topic. Then write down every related idea that occurs to you without judging the value of any of those ideas. Allow ample time for brainstorming as this process may include multiple sessions that span several days. When you feel you have captured most of the ideas, group them into categories. Eliminate those that are redundant.

Review the literature

This step should be initiated during your brainstorming session. Brainstorming and literature review are recursive processes. Ideas from your brainstorm will drive your literature search; reading pertinent papers will stimulate new ideas that you can add to your brainstorm list.

Draw a concept map

A concept map is a diagram that illustrates relationships among ideas. Ideas are stated in boxes with your focus statement(s) contained in the top or central box. Related ideas are linked by arrows in a downward or outward branching hierarchy. Relationship types are specified with phrases such as "determines" or "measures."

Free online programs[6] are available to create concept maps, although sometimes creating one manually helps you organize your thinking better. You can manually create a concept map by placing sticky notes on a whiteboard or wall, or simply by drawing circles and arrows on paper. Creating your map should be an iterative process in which ideas are added and eliminated, and relationships are rearranged until a logical pattern emerges. That pattern will serve as the framework for your narrative.

---

6 Edraw: www.edrawsoft.com/concept-mapping-software.php.
FreeMind: http://freemind.sourceforge.net/wiki/index.php/Main_Page

Create an outline

At first impression, creating both a concept map and an outline seems redundant. It is not. A concept map is where you initially herd your ideas into a corral of coherency. The outline is the final step in organizing your thoughts and the first step of the writing process. Generally, the outline contains more detail. Whereas there is much overlap in a concept map and outline, creating both helps cement the organization of your paper just before you begin writing it. In the long run, that will make the writing process much easier. To keep things simple and clear, the major sections of your concept map and outline can be the major components of a scientific paper (see Appendix).

Focus Statements

A focus statement presents the purpose of the paper. You may need more than one to cover the scope of the paper, but should not include more than three. Focus statements may be in the form of hypotheses or objectives, but your paper should not include both.

- **Hypothesis**: a proposed explanation for an occurrence. It can be essentially conjecture to guide the investigation (a working hypothesis) or highly probable based on established facts. Here is an example of an hypothesis based on established facts: "We hypothesized that, similar to hydrogeomorphic characteristics, riparian vegetation in the Whitewater River network scaled with Horton-Strahler orders."
- **Objective**: a statement framed around measuring change in a condition. For example, "Our objective was to determine if residents knew more than campers about avoiding harm from bears."

Concept Map

Here is the beginning of a concept map created for a paper on scaling relations of riparian vegetation in a stream network.[7] The boxes are components of the paper, the top two being the hypotheses that were tested. Ovals describe relationships among components.

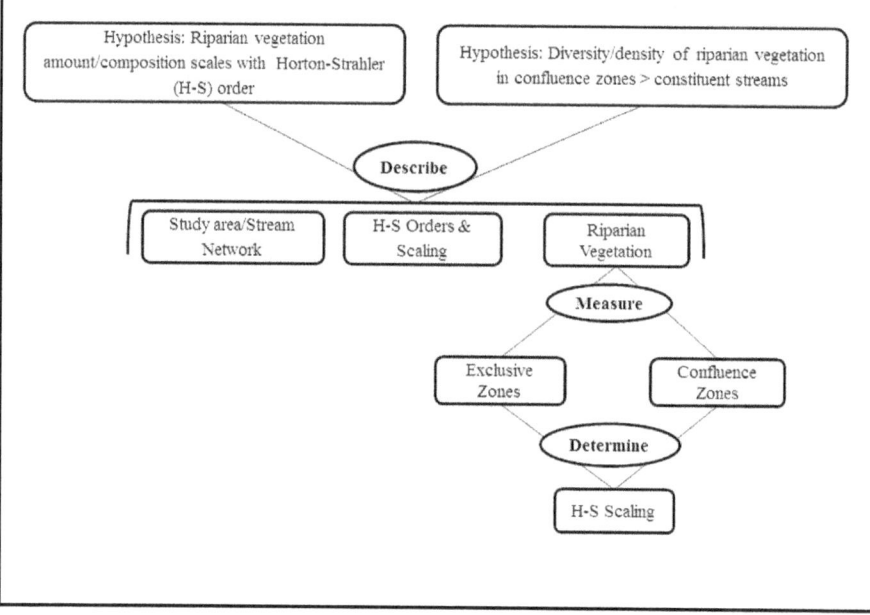

7 Dunn, W. C., B. T. Milne, R. Mantilla, and V. K. Gupta. 2011. Scaling relations between riparian vegetation and stream order in the Whitewater River network, Kansas, USA. Landscape Ecology 26:983-997.

Outline

This outline was created using the components and relationships identified in the above concept map.

I. Introduction
   a. The nature of stream networks
   b. Background on Horton-Strahler (H-S) order and scaling
      i. Hydrogeomorphic variables that scale
      ii. Why riparian vegetation should scale
   c. Hypotheses
      i. Amount and composition of riparian vegetation scales with H-S order.
      ii. Diversity and density of riparian vegetation in confluence zones is greater than along constituent streams.
II. Methods
   a. Description of study area and riverine network
   b. How streams were delineated and classified to H-S order
   c. How riparian vegetation was delineated and classified
      i. GAP habitat types
      ii. Determining accuracy
      iii. Patch classification
   d. Variables that were measured
      i. Exclusive zones: diversity, area, patches (size and shape) of riparian vegetation; stream sinuosity
      ii. Confluence zones: density, diversity of riparian vegetation
III. Results
   a. Data accuracy
   b. Network characteristics
      i. Exclusive zones
      ii. Confluence zones
   c. H-S scaling
      i. Exclusive zones
      ii. Confluence zones

IV. Discussion
    a. Variables that did not scale and why.
    b. Why riparian vegetation scaled with H-S order
        i. Basin area, flow rates, and stable equilibria
        ii. Sinuosity as a feedback mechanism
        iii. Alternative explanations for scaling: conversion of prairie to agriculture
V. Implications for Research and Conservation
    a. Studying self-organizing networks
    b. Measuring water balance
    c. Predicting anthropogenic impacts

Chapter 3. The Written Word

Writing is a great venue for thinking, learning, and teaching. In this section, I focus on a format commonly used in peer-reviewed ecological and conservation journals. It is an excellent framework to help you organize, analyze, and present scientific data with clarity and directness. Many of the techniques, such as how to create tables and figures, will improve clarity for all forms of conservation writing. Personally, I believe natural science students should prepare all papers assigned in their core courses using the framework of peer-reviewed articles (Appendix). By doing so, proper scientific writing would be second nature by the time they become professionals.

The Writing Process

Without a doubt, writing is a lot of work, and to be successful at it requires time, effort, and, most of all, persistence. Here, I discuss an approach to minimize pain and maximize success.

Write your initial draft. Just get words on paper. Don't worry about making your spelling, grammar, or organization perfect. However, as you complete each paragraph, check that the beginning and ending sentences express the subject of the paragraph.

Walk away from it. Take a break if you get to a dead end and cannot think of what you should write next. Walking away is a great way to reset your thinking and may pay dividends in new ideas or perspectives. Given this, I highly recommend you always carry something with you to record thoughts.

Wait...stay with it! On the other hand, if the ideas and words are flowing, keep writing until you finish the paper, drop from exhaustion, or the flow dries up.

Arghh! Writer's Block![8]

It happens to us all—the words just won't flow. Here are some tips to help break through the block.

- Review your concept map and outline.
- Finish this sentence: "What I really mean is..."
- Take a walk and change your scenery; a new visual perspective may lead to a new mental perspective.
- Write at least something every day.
- Talk it out with a friend or even with yourself (but talk to yourself in private!).
- Lower your standards: just get words on paper even if they are slop.
- Don't procrastinate: give yourself enough time to work through the block.

Revise it. Consider revision a continuous process. There is no requirement that you need to revise the entire paper in one sitting. I generally incorporate new ideas or changes as soon as they occur to me. However, there are several keys to making the most of the revision process.

Begin with organization. Move sections and paragraphs of the paper so the order matches your outline. However, don't be afraid

---

8 Johnson-Sheehan, R., and C. Paine. 2010. Writing today. Second edition. Prentice Hall. Upper Saddle River, New Jersey, USA.

to change the order if it improves organization, logic, and flow. But first examine the change on your concept map and outline.

Work on one section, and one paragraph within that section, at a time. Some paragraphs or sentences will be spot-on perfect as soon as you write them. Others will need to be revised several times. Each successive revision should contain a diminishing number of problems to solve. Upon revising an important paragraph, read that section of the paper through to the end of the paragraph. Determine if the ideas and information flow logically and fit well with the rest of the paper.

Transition from big changes to small details. With each revision, your focus should slowly transition from content and organization to spelling, grammar, and sentence structure. However, it's OK to fix a few minor grammatical problems during each revision. This is an especially good way to obtain a feeling of accomplishment when writing is difficult.

Read your paper aloud to yourself. This can help you locate problems in organization, content, flow, and wording.

Have it peer-reviewed. When you have a fairly clean draft, have a colleague or fellow student review your paper. By this point you are probably reading right past some mistakes. Another set of eyes will provide a fresh perspective. Discuss all comments made by your reviewer(s) so you clearly understand all their suggestions. You are not obligated to make all suggested changes, but always be open to improvements.

Direct and Clear

Your audience should be able to easily understand and accurately interpret your writing. That requires direct wording and correct terminology. This section contains three tools to help you with this. First are several tips for improving sentence structure. Next, I list phrases with superfluous wording and provide more direct substitutes. Lastly, I list commonly misused words and provide correct definitions.

Improving sentence structure

<u>Sentence length = one breath</u>. Most sentences should require about one breath to read aloud. The reader may miss important information if sentences are substantially longer. Conversely, your narrative may seem "choppy" if sentences are consistently shorter.

<u>Use the proper tense</u>. In the Abstract, Methods and Results sections, you report on what has already occurred, so these sections mostly should be written in past tense (Appendix). In the Introduction and Discussion sections, you discuss what is known and what needs to be investigated, so these sections may have a combination of past, present, and future tenses.

<u>Use "subject-verb-object" structure</u>. Make it clear who or what is the subject. Use direct language and an active voice. (That is, the subject is active. It does the action specified by the verb.).

- *Not so good.* The river [object] was visited [verb] by Mary [subject].
- *Much better!* Mary [subject] visited [verb] the river [object].

<u>Use scientific topics (for example, species names), not objects of scientific culture (for example, author names, "data," or "research") as the subject.</u>

- *Not so good.* The data show that bears eat berries.
- *Not so good.* Smith and Johnson (1997) show that bears eat berries.
- *Much better!* Bears eat berries (Smith and Johnson 1997).

14

<u>Be careful starting sentences with "This" or "These."</u> The reader may not know what the subject is unless it is clearly defined in the previous sentence.

<u>It is OK to begin sentences with "I" or "We."</u> First person in scientific writing is acceptable and contributes to clarity and brevity.

- *Not so good.* It was hypothesized that riparian vegetation scaled with stream order.
- *Much better!* We hypothesized that riparian vegetation scaled with stream order.

<u>Use the fewest words possible.</u> Inspect every word in a sentence to see if it is necessary. See Superfluous Words (below) for examples.

- *Not so good.* The dead carcass attracted scavengers.
- *Much better!* The carcass attracted scavengers. (All carcasses are dead!)

<u>Do not dangle participles.</u> Participles are verbs used to modify a noun or noun phrase and therefore play a role similar to an adjective or adverb

- *Not so good.* Working [dangling participle] at my desk, the sudden noise [object] startled [verb] me [subject].
- *Much better!* I [subject] was [verb] startled by a sudden noise [object] while I worked at my desk.

<u>Shrink prepositional phrases.</u> Prepositions show the connection between a noun and another word in the sentence.

- *Not so good.* "To the chagrin of the lazy actor, the director of the play asked him to examine with care the notes of the playwright before embarking on the first rehearsal of the opening scenes."
- *Much better!* "The lazy actor was irritated when the director asked him to carefully examine the playwright's notes before rehearsal."

Eliminate nominalizations. Nominalizations are verbs and adjectives that have been turned into nouns.

- *Not so good.* Employees have an expectation that their bosses will be fair.
- *Much better!* Employees expect their bosses to be fair.

Superfluous words.[9]

Verbose Phrase	Suggested Substitute
in this study we assessed	we assessed
we demonstrated that	we demonstrated
there was a direct	direct
were responsible for	caused
played the role of	were
on the basis of evidence available to date	consequently
in order to provide a basis for comparing to	compare
as a result of	through, by
for the following reasons	because
during the course of this experiment	during the experiment
during the process of	during
during periods when	when
for the duration of the study	during the study
the nature of	(omit by rearrangement)
a large (or small or limited) number of	many (or few)
conspicuous numbers of	many
substantial quantities	much
a majority	most
a single	one
an individual taxon	a taxon
seedlings, irrespective of species	all seedlings
all of the species	all species
various lines of evidence	evidence
they do not themselves possess	they lack
were still present	persisted, survived

---

9 This section and the following (Commonly Misused Words) are both taken with permission from the Wildlife Society's 2008 manuscript guidelines for the Journal of Wildlife Management (no longer available).

the analysis presented in this paper — our analysis

indicating the presence of — indicating

in the absence of — without

a series of observations — observations

may be the mechanism responsible for — may have caused

in a single period of a few hours — in a few hours

occur in areas of North America — are in North America

adjacent transects were separated by at least 20 m — ≥20 m apart

in the vicinity — nearby

separated by a maximum distance of 10 m — 10 m apart

the present-day population — the population

their subsequent fate — their fate

whether or not — whether

summer months — summer

are not uncommon — may be

due to the fact that — (omit by rearrangement)

showed a tendency toward higher survival — had higher survival

devastated with drought-induced desiccation — killed by drought

A total of 20 — Twenty

Commonly misused words.

accuracy (see **precision**): noun. Extent of correctness of a measurement or statement.

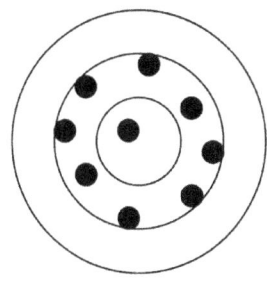
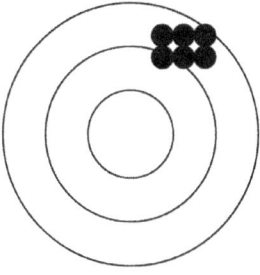
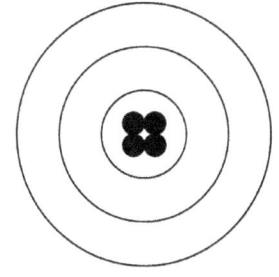

Accurate, not precise   Precise, not accurate   Accurate and precise

affect (see **effect**): verb. To cause a change or an effect; to influence.

among (see **between**): preposition. Use in comparing more than two things. "The money was divided among four players."

between (see **among**): preposition. Use in comparing only two things. "The agreement was between Steve and Bill."

circadian: adjective. Approximately twenty-four hours.

conterminous: adjective. Having a common boundary; meeting at the ends without an intervening gap.

continual: adjective. Going on in time with no, or brief, interruption.

continuous: adjective. Going on in time or space without interruption.

contiguous: adjective. In close proximity; may or may not come in contact.

decimate: verb. To destroy a great number or proportion of.

desiccate: verb. To dry up; to drain of emotion or intellectual vitality.

diurnal: adjective. Recurring every twenty-four hours; occurring in daylight hours.

effect: (see **affect**): usually a noun. The result of an action. As a verb (rare): to bring about or cause to exist, or to perform.

e.g. (see **i.e.**): for example.

enable (see **permit**): verb. To supply with means, knowledge, or opportunity; to make possible.

ensure (see **insure**): verb. To make certain or guarantee.

farther (see **further**): adverb. More distant in space, time, or relationship.

fluctuation: verb. Continual change from one point or condition to another; undulation.

further (see **farther**): adverb. Going beyond what exists, to move forward.

i.e. (see **e.g.**): that is.

incidence (see **prevalence**): noun. Number of cases *developing* per unit of population per unit of time.

insure (see **ensure**): verb. To assure against loss.

logistic: adjective. Symbolic logic.

logistics: noun. Operational details of a project or activity.

mass (see **weight**): noun. A measure of the amount of material an object contains. Used in scientific literature instead of "weight."

percent: adjective, adverb, or noun. Use the word in most cases and always when used as an adjective. Use the symbol ("%") when presenting scientific data. In all cases present the value as a numeral.

percentage: noun. Part of a whole expressed in hundredths; often misused as an adjective. For example, the correct term is "percent error," not "percentage error."

permit (see **enable**): verb. To allow, to give formal consent.

precision (see **accuracy**): degree of refinement with which a measurement is made or stated; for example, the number 3.43 shows more precision than 3.4 but is not necessarily more accurate.

prevalence: (see **incidence**): noun. Number of cases *existing* per unit of population at a given time.

sensu: adverb. As understood or defined by; used in taxonomic references.

since: adverb. From some past time until present; not a synonym for "because" or "as."

presently: adverb. In the future. Not synonymous with "at present" or "currently."

principal (see **principle**): adjective. First in rank or importance.

principle (see **principal**): noun. Accepted rule of conduct; primary laws or truths, such as the laws of physics.

that (see **which**): pronoun introducing a restrictive clause (never immediately preceded by a comma). Example: The lawn mower that is broken is in the garage (tells us which lawnmower is being discussed).

usage: noun. Firmly established and generally accepted practice or procedure.

utilization, utilize: avoid by writing "use" instead.

various: adjective. Of different kinds.

varying: verb. Changing or causing to change. Do not use for "different."

very: adjective. A vague qualitative term; avoid in scientific writing.

weight (see **mass**): noun. The attraction of an object to a body by gravitational force. This term is seldom used in scientific literature.

which (see **that**): pronoun introducing a nonrestrictive clause (often preceded by a comma or preposition [*for, in,* or *of which*]); the word most often misused in professional manuscripts. Example: The lawn mower, which is broken, is in the garage (adds a fact about the lawn mower).

while: conjunction. During the time. Use for *time relationships* but not as synonym for "whereas," "although," or "similarly," which do not imply time.

Tables and Figures[10]

Tables and figures provide information to support statements made in the body of the paper. They are *not* replacements for any part of the narrative but tools to provide clarity. Each should be able to stand alone. In other words, the information in them can be understood in the absence of the rest of the paper. The only exception is when there is a metric that requires more than a brief explanation. In such cases, refer in the legend to the complete explanation that is in the body of the paper.

Guidelines

1. Keep tables and figures simple.
2. Tables should contain no vertical and only three horizontal lines: under the legend, under the column headings, and at the bottom of the table.
3. Place legends above tables and below figures.

---

10 Figures are graphs, photographs, and maps. In scientific papers, they are all labeled "figures."

4. Legends for tables and figures of data should contain three items: **what** was measured, **where** it was measured, and **when** it was measured.
5. Include units of measure in the legend or parenthetically in the column heading.
6. Identify tables and figures by number, not letter, in the order in which they are referred in the body of the paper.
7. In most cases, refer to tables and figures parenthetically in the narrative. They are *not* the subject of the sentence.
   - *Not so good.* "Table 1 shows the results of the study."
   - *Much better!* "Eagles have longer talons than parrots (Table 1)."

Examples

Table

What was measured.

When it was measured.

Where it was measured.

Table 2. Time since residents and campers in New Mexico received information about safety in bear country. Data were collected during 2001–02 at two treatment (information was given to the public) and three control sites (information was not given to the public). Treatment sites included the northern Sangre de Cristo Mountains and the northern Sacramento Mountains. Control sites included the central Sangre de Cristo Mountains, the southern Sacramento Mountains, and the southern Gila National Forest. Values are percent of group totals; sample sizes are in parentheses.

Units of measure

...e information was received	Resident—Control	Resident—Treatment	Camper—Control	Camper—Treatment
<3 months	15.4 (266)	23.2 (300)	18.0 (50)	48.6 (186)
3–12 months	15.7 (272)	25.2 (326)	12.6 (35)	7.6 (29)
1–2 years	13.8 (239)	17.8 (230)	12.2 (34)	12.0 (46)
>2 years	20.3 (352)	14.3 (184)	25.5 (71)	19.6 (75)
Never	34.7 (599)	19.5 (251)	31.7 (88)	12.3 (47)

Three horizontal and no vertical lines. Clean and neat!

Figure

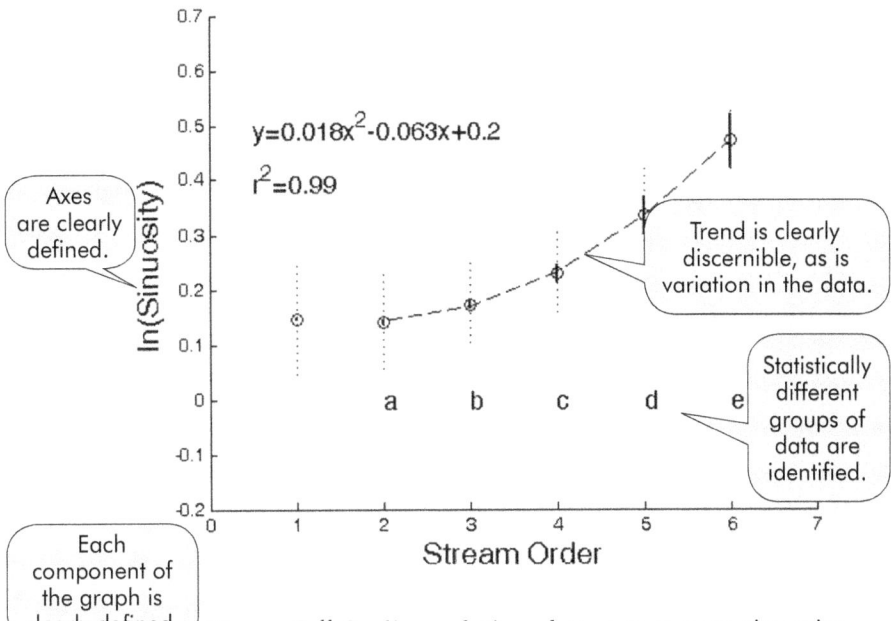

Figure 6. [11] Scaling relations between stream sinuosity and Horton-Strahler orders in the Whitewater River network, Kansas, USA. Open circles represent the natural log of the means for each order. The thick dashed line represents the regression fit for Horton-Strahler orders 2 through 6. Solid and dotted vertical lines represent 95% confidence intervals and standard deviations, respectively. Different letters denote differences in means among orders. The regression equation and coefficient of determination are shown in the upper left of the graph. See Methods for explanation of how sinuosity was calculated.

11 Dunn, W. C., B. T. Milne, R. Mantilla, and V. K. Gupta. 2011. Scaling relations between riparian vegetation and stream order in the Whitewater River basin, Kansas, USA. Landscape Ecology 26:983-997.

23

Citing Literature

Citing literature provides the foundation and justification for ideas, theories, and facts you present in your paper. It is necessary to establish credibility for your paper, and it honors the writing and research of others. Citations should provide enough information for the reader to readily confirm, evaluate, and locate references as needed. Below are formats commonly used in journals of The Wildlife Society and Ecological Society of America for citing literature in the body of a paper and for recording information in the Literature Cited section. Included are examples of common types of citations. How to record other types of citations are shown in the *Journal of Wildlife Management* guidelines (see "Resources" below). If you are submitting an article to a journal, refer to the author guidelines for the specific format they require.

In the body of the paper

Cite literature parenthetically if possible. Like tables and figures, the citation is not the subject of your sentence. Citations include the last name(s) of the author(s) and year of publication with a space between the author name(s) and the year.

Multiple authors: For two authors, cite both names (Russell and Williams 1982). For more than two authors, cite the last name of the first author followed by "et al." Instead of (Kiett, Urban, and Milne 1997), use (Kiett et al. 1997).

Cite more than one source for the same information in chronological order.

Example: Fat reserves average < 5% of the body weight of grouse, so daily foraging is critical to meeting energy needs (Thomas and Popko 1981, Thomas 1982, Dehaley and Moss 1996).

When a sentence provides more than one piece of information. Place sources with the information that they provide.

Example: Range expansion occurs incrementally during fall through natal dispersal (Pitman et al. 2006) and during spring through establishment of new leks by subordinate males (Dunn and Braun 1985, Haukos and Smith 1999).

In the literature cited section

Author names. Cite the first author by last name first, and then initials of his or her first and middle names (with a space between them). Cite subsequent authors by the initials of their first and middle names followed by last names. Commas should be placed between author names.

Citing a source with more than eleven authors. Use the first author's name and initials, followed by "et al."

Separating parts of the citation. Use a period followed by two spaces.

Capitalize only the first word of the title of the article, book, or book chapter.

Indentation. Use hanging indents of five spaces. (In MS Word 2010, you can create this formatting via the following path: Home >Paragraph>Special>Hanging).

Citing journal articles. Spell out the title of the journal. Follow the title of the journal with the volume and page numbers of the article. Include the issue number only if page numbering is not continuous with the last issue.

Citing books. Spell out the name and location of the publisher.

Examples

Journal Article

Van Den Bussche, R. A., D. Wolfe, and S. K. Sherrod. 2003. Genetic variation within and among fragmented populations of lesser prairie-chickens. (*Tympanuchus pallidicinctus*). Molecular Ecology 12: 675–683.

Book

Allen, T. F. H., and T. B. Starr. 1982. Hierarchy: perspectives for ecological complexity. The University of Chicago Press, Chicago, Illinois, USA.

Chapter in a Book

Schlesinger, W. H. 1986. Changes in soil carbon storage and associated properties with disturbance and recovery. Pages 194–220 *in* J. R. Trabalka and D. E. Reichle, editors. The changing carbon cycle: a global analysis. Springer Verlag, New York, New York, USA.

Government Publication

Thomey, M. L., P. L. Ford, M. C. Reeves, D. M. Finch, M. E. Litvak, and S. L. Collins. 2014. Review of climate change impacts on future carbon stores and management of warm deserts of the United States. General Technical Report RMRS-GTR-316. U. S. Forest Service, Rocky Mountain Research Station, Ft. Collins, CO, USA.

Online Source

Hagen, C. A., and K. M. Giesen. 2005. Lesser prairie-chicken (*Tympanuchus pallidicinctus*) *in* A. Poole, editor. The birds of North America online. <http://bna.birds.cornell.edu/bna/species/364> Accessed 15 March 2014.

Six Final Thoughts

1. **You and your words: a nice acquaintance, not a marriage.** The harder you work on getting words on paper, the less willing you are to give them up. Fight that feeling! The first draft is never

the final draft; revision is part of the process. All words, sentences, and paragraphs should be fodder for improvement.

2. **Brevity is next to godliness.** Yes, I know the correct phrase is "cleanliness is next to godliness." My point is to *get to the point.* Your readers are busy and, just like you, have a lot of thoughts competing for their attention. Your goal is to provide pertinent information about the subject in a compelling and interesting way. Delete information that you would *like* to share but your reader doesn't *need* to know.

Getting to the Point: A Lesson from History[11] [12]

> Do you know who gave the Gettysburg Address?
> Sorry, that's not correct.
>
> Edward Everett, a prominent statesman and great orator of the Civil War era, was invited to give the keynote address at the dedication of the cemetery at Gettysburg. Abraham Lincoln was essentially no more than a "ribbon cutter" with his role limited to a few brief dedicatory remarks. Yet, after the ceremony, Everett told Lincoln that the three-minute (272 word) speech of the president summarized the importance of the occasion much better than Everett's own two hours (*13,607 words!*) of oratory.
>
> Lincoln's words are some of the most quoted
> in American history.
> Can you recall *anything* that Everett said?
> I can't either.

---

11 Wills, G. 1992. Lincoln at Gettysburg: the words that remade America. Simon and Schuster, New York, New York, USA.

12 Holzer, H. 1999. Lincoln's flat failure?: the Gettysburg myth revisited. Pages 33–46 *in* J. Y. Simon, H. Holzer, and W. D. Pederson, editors. The Lincoln Forum: Abraham Lincoln, Gettysburg, and the Civil War. Savas Publishing Company, Mason City, Iowa. USA.

3. **Writing requires thinking.** A paper comprised mainly of generalities with little detail usually means the writer did not adequately think about the subject matter. Ask (and answer!) probing questions as you write and revise. Good writing takes concentration. To facilitate this, find a quiet environment where the phone isn't ringing, people aren't talking, and music isn't playing.

4. **Writing is hard work.** Poor grammar, sentence structure, and organization are evidence of a lack of effort. Stay rested and well fed during the writing process. In addition, stay disciplined. Write for set periods of time (say one hour) and then give yourself a twenty-minute break. Exception: If the words are flowing, stay with it until you are finished or the momentum slows down.

5. **Best friends forever: you, a dictionary, and the *Chicago Manual of Style*.** Have these resources readily accessible, and refer to them frequently as you write. Master what the *Chicago Manual of Style* says.

6. **Be a better reader to become a better writer.** You can gain a lot of ideas on style, sentence structure, and use of words by regularly reading professional papers in your discipline. Any reading (even an occasional checkout-stand magazine!) can improve your mastery of the English language.

Chapter 4. The Spoken Word

Being able to effectively speak to the public can be an important tool for gaining support to achieve professional goals. By "public" I mean all persons and organizations interested or affected by what you do or produce. The thought of speaking to an audience often elicits fear and trepidation. In particular, there are concerns about boring or confusing the audience, saying something that results in negative reactions, or making an erroneous statement. In reality, there is no need to be inordinately fearful. Oral presentations are an outstanding method of participating in a two-way exchange of information and ideas if they are done right. This means that your presentation should be:

- **Informative:** It provides all necessary information to convey your main point.
- **Creative:** It is interesting to see and hear. The format and graphics contribute to understanding the information you convey.
- **Compelling:** It commands attention and respect.
- **Thought provoking:** It elicits new ways to think about your subject, and it results in constructive ideas from your audience.

Oral presentations encompass four forms of communication: the posture and movement of your body (in other words, body language), the inflection and cadence of your voice, the words you say, and the visual aids you use. In this section are lessons to improve each form. Specifically, I address how to (1) structure an effective presentation, (2) create clear and informative visual graphics, and (3) speak so your message is well received.

For some, public speaking simply is not a natural gift, and incorporating the lessons that follow will not change that fact. However, what these lessons can do is improve the craft of oral presentation so that it does not detract from other strengths you possess. My desire is that you will develop your ability to speak before audiences so that your oral presentations make a positive contribution for conservation.

Find Your Boundaries

Key to an effective presentation is staying within the boundaries of time, format, and culture. So, before creating any presentation, always obtain information about the following:

How much time? Find out how much time you have to speak and *never, ever* speak longer than that. Your real time limit should be **75 percent** of the allotted time so there is adequate time for questions and discussion. Why? The value of most presentations is not just in providing information but in receiving it as well. Your presentation may take up most of the allotted time, but the greatest benefit to you may be questions and comments from your audience.

What is the format? Will your talk generally be informal with comments and questions from the audience during the presentation, or will it be a formal presentation in which the audience participates only after you have spoken? What is the anticipated size of the audience, how large is the venue, and what amenities (computers, projectors, version of PowerPoint) will your host offer? Of critical importance is making sure your presentation is compatible with the version of PowerPoint that the host provides.

Who is your audience? Identify the cultural, social, and educational characteristics of your audience as well as their wants and needs. You can obtain information about your audience from the person who invited you, by reading information published by the organization, and by studying their website. Specifically, determine their knowledge and perceptions about your subject. Use this information to frame your presentation. Importantly, set your message to their level of understanding. For example, if you are presenting research results to the general public, avoid using complex equations that require advanced scientific expertise to comprehend. Conversely, for an audience of seasoned scientists, only include basic concepts if they are needed to set a foundation for more advanced aspects of your topic.

Structure

Determining what you will say and the order you will present your information essentially follows the same steps as those used to develop a written document. One additional step is to include in your outline brief descriptions of slides that you will use.

The structure of your presentation should follow the hourglass model (in other words, broad, specific, broad). Thus, the introduction should provide a *broad* overview of the subject on which you will speak and your focus statement(s) to set the direction of your presentation. The body of the presentation should be where you zoom in and provide *specific* information about the methods and results, particularly pertinent information from other studies. The discussion and conclusion should provide a *broad* view, putting the presentation into the context of what it contributes to science and conservation. Importantly, offer one to three important findings that address your focus statement(s). Also mention what still needs to be investigated; good research often yields more questions than it answers.

Graphics and Visual Aids

The advent of Microsoft PowerPoint and similar programs has provided an exponential increase in opportunities for creativity in oral presentations. However, this has been both a blessing and a curse. The blessing has come in providing more ways to help audiences assimilate the information you provide. The curse comes from using too many gimmicks that result in the gimmicks, not the information shared, becoming the center of attention. The key to effectively using PowerPoint as part of an oral presentation is to keep your slides clean and simple. You want your audience to concentrate on your message, not on trying to decipher confusing, cluttered slides. In other words, **do not allow your slides to compete against you for the attention of your audience!** In this section, I present guidelines and provide examples of proper design.

Slide design: the ten things you really need to know

Background. Choose colors that are neutral and patterns that are muted. There is nothing wrong with a plain white background. Use only one background type per presentation.

Font. Words should be large enough to be clearly read from the back of the room. Choose a font that is simple, clear, and pleasant to the eyes (I generally use Calibri or Tahoma, 24 to 36 point). Choose a color that contrasts well with the background color of the slide. Use capitalization, bold print, or italics only to emphasize really important points.

Make This Your New Career Goal

During a presentation **never, ever** say, "I know you can't see what is on this slide but..."

If they can't see it, why are you showing it?

Content. One (and only one!) subject per slide.

Bullet statements. Follow my "3–25" rule for bullet statements. For each slide, include no more than twenty-five words contained within no more than three bullets. Convert sentences to short phrases of key words. Use multiple slides if the subject matter requires more bullet points.

Maps. Include maps only if the specific location of your study is relevant to your presentation. Show only landmarks needed to orient the viewer. Make sure all labels and symbols are large enough to see from the back of the room.

Tables. Tables represent the biggest opportunity to fail at achieving your new career goal (see box above). Strive to limit table size to nothing larger than four by four cells.

Numbers. Present only pertinent data that emphasize big differences. Use round numbers. Avoid using decimal points unless necessary.

Graphs. Show trends clearly. Minimize the number of categories. Include only the numbers needed to show the trend.

Photographs. One picture is worth a thousand words but only if the audience can see it and only if it adds to the point you are trying to make. Use only clear, well-composed, relevant photographs.

Other visual aids. Use them sparingly. If you embed a video in your PowerPoint presentation, keep it short and make certain it works. Keep physical aids (for example, equipment used in the study) few in number and easy to present. Do not distribute handouts during the presentation; it is distracting.

Examples

<u>Title Slide</u>

What You Need to Notice

- The title is clear and to the point. Its font is large enough (36 point) to be read from the back of the room.
- The background color is muted and visually pleasant (albeit a bit bland in this example!).
- The photograph is clear and well-composed. The subject is clearly related to the theme of presentation.
- Author names, affiliations, and contact information are provided.

Presentation Outline

Safety in Bear Country
What We Will Discuss

I. Introduction: The problem, the hypotheses

II. Methods: "Us to them," "Them to us"

III. Results: What did the public know?

IV. Discussion: What does it mean for management?

What You Need to Notice

- The outline is an essential component. It helps set the direction for your presentation.
- For the most part, limit your outline to major sections only (I, II, etc.).

Introduction: The Scope of the Problem

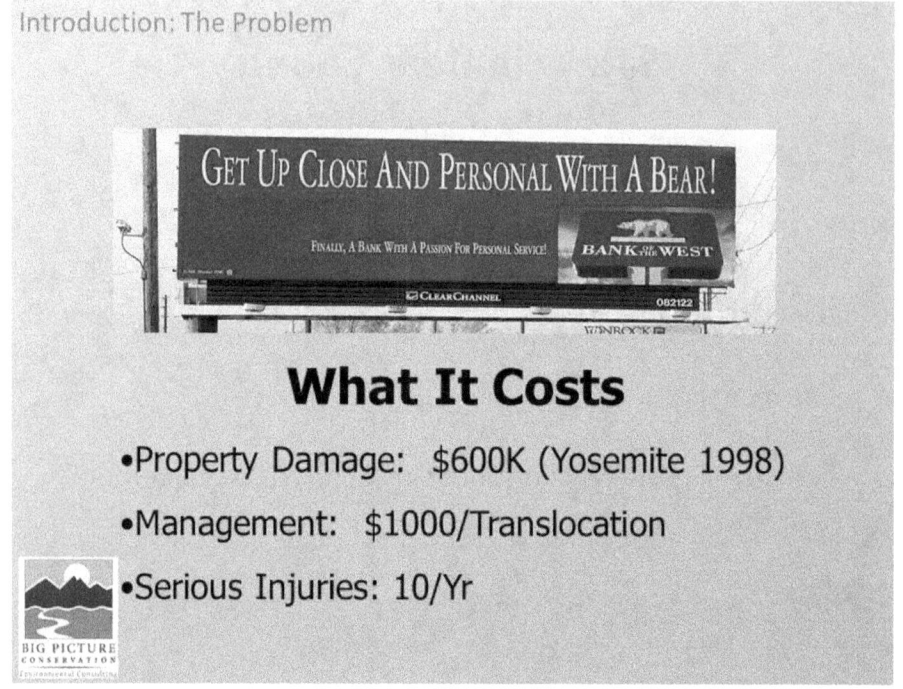

What You Need to Notice

- Your place in the presentation is identified in the upper left corner.
- The picture is of a commonly seen advertisement whose theme is pertinent to the topic. It serves to capture the attention of the audience.
- Values are presented as round numbers for clarity.

<u>Study Area Map</u>

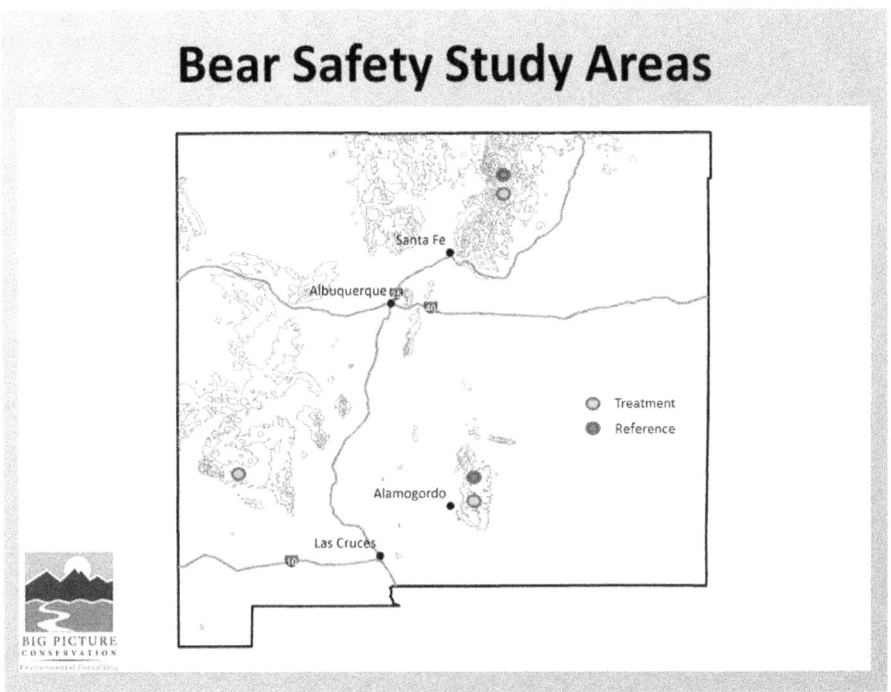

What You Need To Notice

- Landmarks are limited to four towns and interstate highways—just enough to orient the viewer.
- Mountainous areas are identified by simple contours.
- Study areas are clearly identified; the legend is simple and clear.

Focus Statements

Introduction: Hypotheses

Who Knows More?

1. H_o: Residents = Campers

2. H_o: People provided information =

    People not provided information

BIG PICTURE
CONSERVATION

What You Need to Notice

- The wording of these hypotheses is as simple as it gets. But remember, your slides *should* be simple and clear. Their job is to complement, not repeat, what you are saying.

Methods

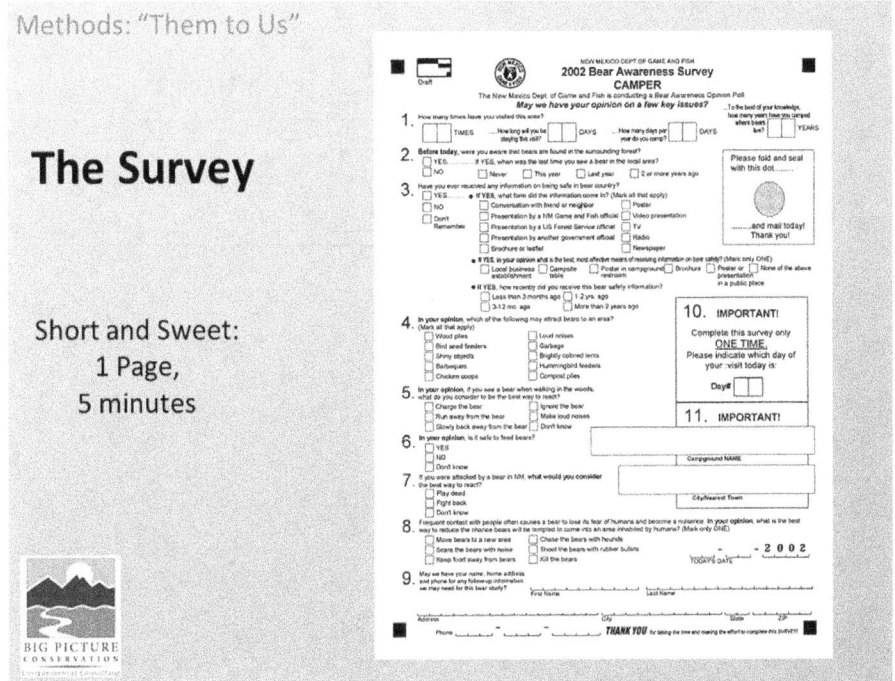

Methods: "Them to Us"

The Survey

Short and Sweet:
1 Page,
5 minutes

What You Need to Notice

- OK, OK! I know you can't read the words on the survey form and that contradicts the Career Goal I set out for you. However, this represents the one exception to the rule— when the focus is not the words but the object that contains the words (in this case, a one-page form).
- "Short and Sweet": A nice, concise synopsis of a nice, concise survey.

Tables

Do not do this…

Riparian Vegetation of the Whitewater River

Table 2. Riparian vegetation types in the Whitewater River basin, Kansas (from Egbert et al. 2001).

Vegetation Type	Exclusive zones			Area in intersect zones (ha)	Total area (ha)	Dominant Species
	Number of patches	Mean patch size (ha ± SD)	Area (ha)			
Pecan Floodplain Forest	152	0.35±0.84	53.6	54.6	108.2	Carya illinoiensis, Celtis occidentalis, Acer negundo
Ash-Elm-Hackberry Floodplain Forest	347	0.52±4.7	179.3	2361.5	3984.8	Fraxinus pennsylvanicus, Ulmus sp., C. occidentalis, Juglan nigrum
Cottonwood Floodplain Forest	146	0.39±1.3	567.2	526.2	1096.4	Populus deltoides, Planus occidentalis, A. negundo
Cottonwood Floodplain Woodland	784	0.46±1.18	322.2	260.8	583.0	P. deltoides, Salix nigra, A. negundo
Willow Shrubland	55	0.35±0.4	10.3	1.2	11.2	Salix exigua, Andropogon gerardii
Low or Wet Prairie	385	0.32±0.83	121.5	117.9	239.4	Spartina pectinata, Eleocharis sp.
Cattail Marsh	939	0.51±1.07	287.9	248.9	536.8	Typha sp., Eleocharis sp.
Total	722	-	315.0	3371.0	6527.0	

BIG PICTURE
CONSERVATION
Environmental Consulting

…but instead do this.

Riparian Vegetation

Veg Type	Area (ha)	No. Patches	Patch Size (ha)
Ash-Elm	4000	3500	0.6
Cottonwood	1600	2200	0.4
Shrub	800	1300	0.24

BIG PICTURE
CONSERVATION

What You Need to Notice

- The table meets the recommended size of 4 x 4 cells.
- The font is large and easy to read.
- Column titles are clear and succinct.
- Only the most important groups are shown.
- Groups are ordered from highest to lowest values so trends are clear.
- Values are presented as round numbers.

Figures

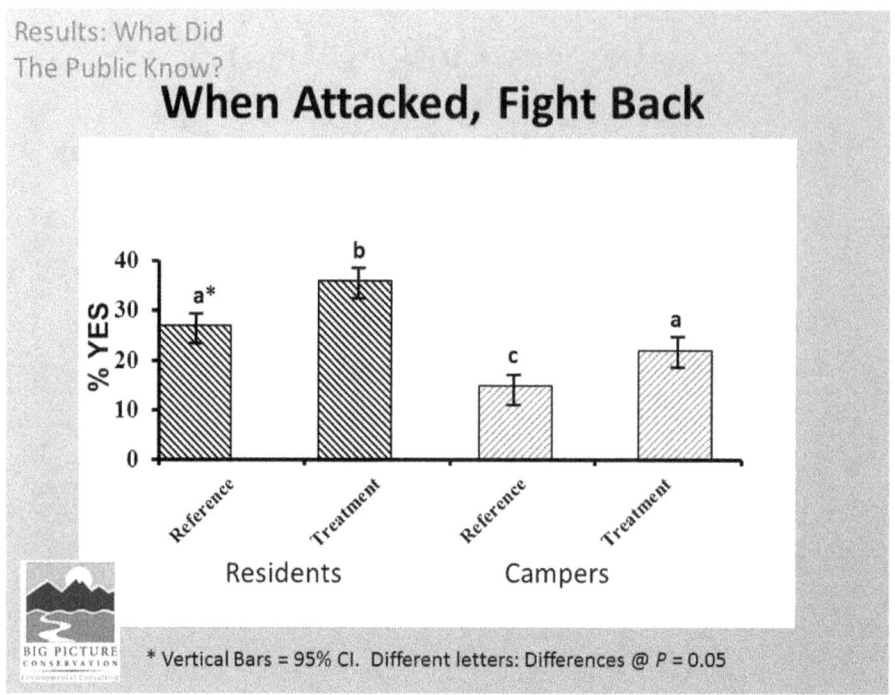

What You Need to Notice

- Only major delineations of the Y axis (10% increments) are shown. Also the font is large for easy reading.
- Bars are large and easy to differentiate.
- Definitions of differences among groups are given at the bottom of the slide. This is optional; you may want to just verbally state how differences are defined.

Synthesis and Conclusions

Discussion: What Does It Mean?

Take-Home Messages

- Foundational Knowledge Exists
  - *i.e., Food is Bad*

- Public Education Works
  - *Contributing Factor: Exposure to the Problem*

- It's Cheap: *$200/Campground*

What You Need to Notice

- This is the mission critical "big picture." If they forget everything else you say (hopefully not though), this is what you really need them to remember. To achieve success, limit your list to no more than three items.

Acknowledgments

Acknowledgments

L. Fisher, U. S. Forest Service

R. Winslow, NM Dept. Game and Fish

Funding: USFWS Federal Aid in Wildlife Restoration Project W93-R33.

BIG PICTURE
CONSERVATION

Contact:
Bill@BigPictureConservation.com

What You Need to Notice

- *Always* honor those who fund you.
- Contact information should be the last item provided in the presentation.

Your Talk

Getting ready

Complete your slides and notes one week before your presentation. Your notes should be phrases comprised of key words, not complete sentences. Use one 3x5 card for each slide, or numerically list notes for each slide on a sheet of paper or in digital format. Font size should be large enough to be easily read.

Who are you? Prepare a brief (one short paragraph) biographic sketch of yourself for the host to use in introducing you. Include education, experience, and one unique aspect that connects you to the subject of your presentation.

Practice, practice, practice!!! Everyone says it, and there are good reasons why. A lot of nuances need to be mastered so your presentation is clear, smooth, and easily understood. Ideally, you should practice enough that you have achieved the following by the time you speak to your audience:

- *Eliminate jargon and bureaucratic buzzwords; minimize acronyms and abbreviations.* Jargon, buzzwords, acronyms, and abbreviations might contribute to brevity when communicating with coworkers, but they can be a source of confusion to your audience. Use an acronym or abbreviation only if the term it replaces is cumbersome and is used more than three times in the presentation. Define the acronym or abbreviation the first time you use it.
- *Minimize technical terms, and ensure they are well defined.* Clear definitions are needed because terms may have different meanings to different groups.
- *Don't apologize, but do qualify.* Do not apologize for your findings. They are what they are, and apologies only distract from your message. Conversely, do not overstate the value

of what you found. I recommend choosing among three qualifiers depending on data strength. Use "suggest" if you find an explainable pattern to your data, but your sample size is small, your data suffer from poor precision or accuracy[13], and few other studies have produced similar results. Use "indicate" if the patterns of your data and differences among groups being compared are evident and explainable, you have a good sample, data are reasonably accurate and precise, and similar findings have been reported by some other studies. Use "demonstrate" if you have a large sample size of precise, accurate data, patterns in the dataset are clear, large differences among groups being compared are evident and similar findings have been reported in several other studies.

- *Eliminate distracting mannerisms.* You shouldn't stand stone still, but unneeded movements should be minimized. Keep both hands out of your pockets; even keeping one hand in a pocket creates an imbalance in your appearance. Do not grasp the top of the podium with both hands; it signals defensiveness. However, stay at or near the podium; do not pace around the stage.
- *Maintain a confident appearance.* Stand tall, keep your head erect, and look out toward your audience.
- *Use laser pointers appropriately.* Use them only to emphasize important data or patterns. Practice enough to ensure a steady hand.
- *Ensure that there are no unneeded interruptions in flow.* Eliminate stuttering, unneeded repetition of words or statements, unplanned pauses, and mental space savers, such

---

13 Accuracy: correctness of a measurement or statement. Precision: resolution with which a measurement is made or stated. For example, if the true value of something is 3.5, the estimate 3.33 is more precise, but the estimate 3.4 is more accurate.

as "OK," "uh," or "umm." However, I do recommend one interruption— namely to pause momentarily and take a deep breath between slides to reset your composure.

- *Make minimal use of notes.* But have them ready just in case.
- *Develop a compelling speaking style.* The pattern and tone of your speech should reflect a sincere interest in your subject, but keep the interest within the confines of a professional demeanor. Displaying evangelistic fervor may bring your objectivity into question.

It is especially important to work on cadence and inflection. Cadence is the rhythm or flow of your presentation. It should be smooth, not halting. Pauses should be appropriately placed to emphasize particularly important statements or to allow the audience to absorb a block of information. Inflection is emphasis represented by changes in pitch and volume of your voice. The words you say are the skeleton of your presentation; the inflection in your voice as you say the words represents the muscle that moves your presentation. Without inflection, your presentation will be a lifeless pile of bones. Practice so the proper amount of emphasis is given to the appropriate words.

A Few Words about Inflection

Getting inflection right is important because it affects interpretation. In fact, the number of interpretations of a sentence is equal to the number of words that comprise it. I illustrate this principle with the emphasis of each word of the sentence "Joe loves big cats."

"*Joe* loves big cats."　　　Joe is one person whom we are sure loves big cats.

"Joe *loves* big cats."　　　Joe has a unique and special affinity for big cats.

"Joe loves *big* cats."　　　The size of the cat is of special importance to Joe.

"Joe loves big *cats*."　　　Joe's interest is in cats, not just any big animal.

- *Make sure your presentation is the right length.* I can't say this enough, so I will say it again: stay within 75 percent of your allotted time!
- *Pass muster with your peers.* Practice at least a few times in front of friends or colleagues. Consider their ideas for improving your presentation.

The day arrives

Before the meeting

- *Show up well rested.* There should be no need to deprive yourself of sleep the night before your presentation if you completed your slides and notes the week before and prepared well during the intervening period.
- *Dress appropriately and look professional.* For the most part, dress to match your audience. A suit may be in order if speaking to business professionals but is overkill if addressing ranchers. The lowest threshold for any presentation should be nice jeans, a button-down shirt, and casual shoes (*never* sneakers!).
- *Know your environment.* Get to the venue well before the meeting begins. Stand where you will be speaking and survey the layout of the room. Make sure all equipment is working properly and the environment (room temperature, background noise, air circulation, lighting) is comfortable. Do not be afraid to ask your host for changes to the room environment if it will enhance audience comfort.
- *Chat up your audience.* Grab a cup of coffee at the refreshment table, and engage in casual conversation with members of the audience that are milling about. It relaxes you and offers the opportunity to assess their mood and mind-set.

You're up!

- *Be aware of the state of your audience.* If you are scheduled near the end of a long symposium, don't be afraid to invite your audience to briefly stand up and stretch before you begin your presentation.
- *Change slides yourself.* Giving verbal cues is distracting.
- *Speak up and speak out.*
  - The back of the room is your target. Everything on your slides should be clearly seen, and everything you say should be clearly heard at the back of the room.
  - Speak to the audience, not to your slides. You can glance at your slide on the podium computer. Turn toward the slide only if you need to point to an item on it, but do so while maintaining an angle at which the front of your body faces at least part of the audience.
  - Balance your direction. Over the course of your presentation, try to scan equally across the right, center, and left segments of the audience. Then everyone will feel that you are addressing them.
  - Minimize direct eye contact. This may seem contradictory to speaking to the audience, but seeing a negative reaction on the face of a person or in his or her body language can be extremely distracting. For the most part, look across the crowd, not directly at individuals. By doing so, the audience becomes a benign amorphous mass to you, but they perceive that you are making good eye contact with them.
- *Humor.* If you do tell a joke, keep it relevant to the subject, low-key, and short. Absolutely no off-color humor! Practice the joke so you get the cadence and inflection right. Often humor is not in the words but how and when they are said.

- *What if you forget what to say next?* Do not worry about the reaction of your audience. Pause. Breathe. Refer to your notes, or just move on to the next slide.
- *Gulp! Questions and comments from the audience.* Should you answer questions during the presentation? Sometimes yes, but generally no. Find out from the person who invited you what sort of setting to expect. In a classroom seminar or business meeting, a give-and-take atmosphere often is encouraged. Thus, participants may ask questions about a subject at the time it is addressed, and you have the flexibility to answer them. However, in many scientific meetings where you have limited time, answering questions during the presentation may disrupt its flow. If a question is asked in such situations, thank the person and request that he or she waits until the end of the presentation.
    - <u>Suggested transition</u>. "Thank you for your attention. At this time, I would be happy to answer any questions or receive any comments you might have."
    - <u>Repeat the questions</u>. Questioners face you and generally do not have microphones, so many in the room may not hear what they are asking. This also will give you a moment to consider your answer.
    - <u>Return to appropriate slides</u>. If a question is focused on data shown on a particular slide, show that slide to help you provide a clear answer to the question.
    - <u>Know your stuff, and know your audience.</u> A standard line to calm nerves before giving a presentation is "Don't worry. You know the subject better than anyone else in the room." That's a great statement, but only if it is true. Fielding questions is where you find out why it is so critical to know your subject and

audience, and to be able to anticipate what your audience might ask or say in reference to your topic.

- <u>If you don't know the answer, don't guess</u>. No matter how well you prepare, there may be questions for which you have no answer. The solution is simple: just say you don't know. Only speculate as a means of stimulating new thinking, but be clear that it is speculation and nothing more. Then offer to find a better answer in the near future. Ask questioners to give you their contact information after the presentation is completed. Of course, your contact information should be on the screen since it is the last item on your last slide.
- <u>Hostile reactions</u>. Give direct answers. Skirting the issue will only serve to inflame emotions. If needed, offer to discuss the situation further during a break or after the meeting. Remind the questioner of your contact information. Above all, *always* maintain a calm demeanor.

Chapter 5. Special Situations

Informing Decision Makers

Decision makers are those who have authority to provide resources and approve actions to make conservation happen. This group extends from project managers to leaders of companies, nongovernmental organizations, and government agencies. Whatever their level, you can safely assume they are very busy people. On any given day, decision makers, especially senior managers, have a myriad of concerns to address and rarely have the luxury of intensively studying any single issue. Therefore, if you get an audience with them, get to the point. Given this, I recommend two numbers: 1 and 5. The first refers to the maximum number of pages of written correspondence you should send them; the second refers to the maximum number of minutes you should plan on meeting with them in person or via a conference call. These are conservative values, but it is better if a decision maker requests more rather than less input.

The information you provide in either venue should answer four questions: (1) What is the issue? (2) What pertinent background information about the issue does the decision maker need to know? (3) What do you want the decision maker to do about the issue? (4) Why is your proposed solution in the best interest of the organization?

Well before any meeting or conference call, send a synopsis of what you will present so the decision maker(s) can prepare. In addition, anticipate what other information may be needed, and have it available if they request it. After the meeting, send an e-mail to thank the decision makers for their time, provide any additional information requested, and summarize the main points of the meeting.

Public Meetings

Bill Graves, former planner with the New Mexico Department of Game and Fish, often described the two components of communication as "us to them" and "them to us." The "them," of course, are people and organizations interested in or affected by the conservation actions you propose. Most of what has been discussed in this book so far is "us to them." In this section, I focus on how to achieve "them to us" communication through public meetings where the audience provides verbal comments. Here the main role of the conservation professional is that of obtainer, rather than presenter, of information. The main role of the public also shifts from spectator to participant and potential supporter.

In Chapter 1, I stated that most conservation requires public support. After all, when it comes to wildlife or public lands, the public owns the resources. Additionally, many conservation laws require public input. However, there is a world of difference between meeting the letter of the law, and gaining information and support that will enhance your ability to conserve natural resources. Within that mass of people whom we label "the public" resides a wide diversity of perspectives, information, and experience that can help you avoid problems and pitfalls as well as add positive ideas to your project.

Prepare well

If you want to get a lot out of a public meeting, you have to put a lot into it. And much of what you need to put into a meeting occurs well before it begins. Everything that I suggested for a successful oral presentation, from familiarizing yourself with your audience to handling hostile reactions, applies here.

The first step is to determine why you need input and what specific information you would like to obtain. Tools described in "Laying the Foundation," such as the concept map, can help.

Here are some questions to answer as you prepare:
- What specific issues surround the proposed action?
- How will public input help address the issues?
- What information do I need from the public?
- How will I get that information?
- Who is interested or affected by the issues?
- What support or opposition do I anticipate? How will I manage contentious interactions?

Next, create a PowerPoint presentation and materials (printed and web-based) to inform your audience about the topic and to outline (specifically) what information you would like from them. You know the rules: clear, concise, complete. Following the three C's is especially important for public input. Obfuscation can needlessly raise suspicion about underlying motives for your proposed action.

Lastly, announce the meeting in a timely manner and advertise it at venues that ensure you will reach all interested and affected publics. If possible, personally contact the leaders of organizations from whom it is important to obtain views. Announcements should state the topic, provide a brief overview of the issues surrounding the topic, provide the time (starting and ending) and date of the meeting, and state where additional information may be obtained.

Manage the meeting

Begin the meeting. Start on time, and welcome your audience as if they are valued members of your team—because they are. Make sure everyone has had the opportunity to sign in and obtain printed materials about the topic. Introduce yourself by stating your responsibility in the organization you represent and how you are involved in the project. Then present the ground rules, namely how the meeting will proceed and how people will be able to express their views. Emphasize that all views are welcome, but they must be presented in a courteous manner and within the allotted time limit (and don't forget to mention how much time that is). State how audience members can obtain more information and contribute ideas or comments after the meeting (e-mail, website, etc.).

Us to them. Introduce the topic with a short (less than ten minutes) PowerPoint presentation that outlines the essential components of the proposed action and issues surrounding it. The purpose is to focus input so as to minimize questions and comments peripheral to the topic. Discuss the decision-making process for the conservation action, emphasizing how and where the public can be involved.

Them to us.
- *How you record it.* Appoint someone from your organization to record information so you can give your complete attention to those providing input. Use media that allow the audience to clearly see the comments. I recommend a computer, projector, and screen instead of a flip chart because inaccuracies can be easily corrected, poor penmanship does not hinder the process, and all comments can be stored to file as they are made. To allow maximum participation, paraphrase comments instead of recording them verbatim. Read the paraphrase out loud, and ask the

participant if it captures what he or she is saying. If not, ask what needs to be corrected.

- *How they comment.* If verbose, remind them of the time limit as they near it, and stop them when they get to it. If hostile, remind them (calmly, but firmly) that being courteous is a requisite. Hopefully, professional security will not be needed for your meeting, but consider having it readily available if you anticipate an overly contentious atmosphere.
- *Answering questions.* Answer questions to provide factual information but not to offer opinion or speculation. In such cases, politely remind the audience that the purpose of the meeting is to obtain their opinions, not yours.

End the meeting. End on time, but be flexible if a constructive exchange of ideas and information has not yet finished. Conclude the meeting with a brief review of the comments. Then thank everyone for their participation and remind them of subsequent steps in the process, particularly those in which they can participate.

Follow up with participants. Organize comments under applicable issues. Make the comments available on the web. Thank participants via e-mail, inform them where they can obtain comments from the meeting, and announce subsequent events in the decision-making process.

On Being an Effective Participant

Public meetings are a forum for exchanging ideas and sharing information. Here are some tips for effective input if you participate as a member of the public.

- **Come prepared.** Read available printed and web materials on the proposed action and issues surrounding the action. Study the mission, duties, and budget of the organization that is proposing the conservation action. Write down comments and questions that arise from what you read.

- **Keep it short, relevant, and on topic.** When it is your turn to comment, get to the point (and make it a good one) so that others have ample opportunity to participate.

- **Suggest the possible.** Use what you know about the sponsoring organization in framing your comments. Suggesting ideas well outside the mission, budget, and ability of those who will implement the proposed action does not help the decision-making process.

- **Check your emotions.** You want to be remembered for what you say, not how you say it. Tears or outbursts of anger provide no positive contribution. You can show displeasure (or pleasure) but do it in a controlled manner. Just as important, be courteous to others, and do not detract from their comments with an emotional response.

- **Don't cross your arms.** This is a corollary to "Check your emotions." Crossing your arms is a defensive posture that signals anger, disgust, or mistrust. That may be how you feel, but a better way to convey your feelings is with a well-stated comment.

- **Thank your host.** Facilitating public meetings is difficult work. E-mail or write your hosts to thank them for the opportunity to take part—and to remind them of your comments. It just might result in what you said at the meeting getting a closer look.

Chapter 6. The Final Word

Conservation consists of studying nature and then, based on that knowledge, accomplishing actions that restart—or allow continuation of—natural processes. The conduit through which knowledge is transformed into action is built with words. Use the wrong materials (words) or employ a faulty design (how you communicate), and the connection will be weak or not made at all. This book provides the tools to make a strong connection that lasts, and at this point, it should be clear that success in doing so requires a lot of thought and hard work.

Indeed, the challenge was evident from the beginning with an apparent contradiction in the three C's. How is it possible for communication about nature to be complete yet concise? After all, ecosystems are complex, and conserving them can be complicated, especially when you include the interests and emotions of people. It follows that writing or speaking about conservation should require a lot of words to adequately explain the fine points of research or proposed conservation actions.

The key to solving this dilemma is to know your audience and focus your message accordingly. One starting point may be to relate your topic to those interests universal among all Americans— finances and health. Thus, the question to be answered is this: "What is it about the knowledge you gained or the conservation action you proposed that will help your audience be more economically secure and enjoy better health?" There are a multitude of answers: (1) for developers, it is less expensive to maintain a functioning ecosystem than to be forced by law to rebuild a broken one; (2) for ranchers, the best long-term return on investment comes from grazing practices that maintain healthy rangelands; (3) for public health professionals, most medicines originate from wild plants and the continued existence of these plants depends on conserving the ecosystems of which they are a part. Thus, human health is inextricably tied to ecosystem health. The Ecological Society of America has done an excellent job of promoting the value of ecosystem services—what nature provides to humans. The information the society has gathered may benefit you in framing your message.

I have emphasized the necessity of good preparation and hard work for successful communication, and it usually pays off. However, there is never any guarantee of a positive response. Sometimes circumstances outside of your control, such as deeply held beliefs or the emotional state of your audience, prevent success. Nevertheless, you *do* have control over how you present a message. Doing it well at every opportunity will eventually benefit conservation. With that, I hope the lessons of this book will help you increase support for nature and move conservation forward!

Resources

Online

Chicago Manual of Style: http://www.chicagomanualofstyle.com/ (requires subscription).

Dictionary.com: http://dictionary.reference.com/

Block, W. M., F. R. Thompson, D. Hanseder, A. Cox, and A. Knipps. 2011. Journal of Wildlife Management Guidelines. http://joomla.wildlife.org/documents/JWMguidelines2011.pdf

Merriam-Webster Online Dictionary: http://www.merriam-webster.com/

Purdue Online Writing Lab: http://owl.english.purdue.edu/

Research and Documentation Online: http://www.bedfordstmartins.com/catalog/static/bsm/hacker/resdoc/

UC Berkeley Libraries: http://www.lib.berkeley.edu/TeachingLib/Guides/Internet/FindInfo.html

Printed

Covey, S. R. 2012. Franklin Covey style guide: for business and technical communication. Fifth edition. FT Press, Upper Saddle River, New Jersey, USA.

Hacker, D. 2010. A writer's reference. Sixth edition. Bedford/St. Martins, Boston, Massachusetts, USA.

Knisely, K. 2009. A student handbook for writing in biology. W. H. Freeman, Sunderland, Massachusetts, USA.

Kosslyn, S. M. 2007. Clear and to the point. Oxford University Press, New York, New York, USA.

Williams, J. M. 2006. Style: the basics of clarity and grace. Second edition. Pearson/Longman, New York, New York, USA.

Appendix. Structure of a Scientific Paper

The typical scientific paper contains four main sections of narrative known by the acronym IMRAD (Introduction, Methods, Results, and Discussion), plus a summary (abstract), supporting tables and figures, a section on implications of the research (if applicable), and a Literature Cited section. Below is a description of six of the sections. How to create tables and figures and a Literature Cited section are discussed in Chapter 3.

Abstract. What is the *big picture*? The abstract is a summary (usually no more than 250 words) of the focus of your study, what you found, and why the findings are significant. It should not contain literature citations or statistical values. The abstract should be the last section written.

Introduction. What will you *address*? This section contains two parts. The *background* is a broad overview of why the paper needs to be written and what is known about the subject. The *focus statement* is the hypothesis(es) or objective(s) that you will address.

Methods. What did you *do*? The methods section is a description of what you did to gather and analyze data to address the focus statement(s). This includes (in order of presentation) a description of your study area, types of instruments or equipment used, techniques of data collection, and analysis and statistical tests employed. It should be complete enough that someone could read your methods and repeat the same procedure. Sentences should be in the past tense.

Results. What did you *find?* State the pertinent (but not necessarily all) findings. This is not the section to discuss *why* the results turned out the way they did. This is where most tables and figures are referenced. Sentences should be in the past tense.

Discussion. What does it *mean?* The primary purpose of this section is to *synthesize* more than *summarize.* **Do not** rehash results[14]. This is the section where you answer *why* you think the results came out the way they did. It also is an opportunity to compare your results with those of others who worked on the subject before you, explain how your findings contribute to the body of knowledge about this subject, and describe what still needs to be investigated. Subjects should be discussed in the same order in which they appeared in the results. Importantly, this section should tie in with the Introduction by addressing why and how well your results addressed your focus statement(s).

Implications for Conservation and Management. What is the *practical application?* This is an optional section (it also can be the final part of the discussion) for highlighting how the findings of the study might contribute to conservation or the management of natural resources.

---

14 Some authors combine results and discussion into one section. I recommend keeping them separate so that reporting and interpretation of findings can be clearly differentiated.

Index

William C. Dunn is an ecologist and owner of Big Picture Conservation LLC, an environmental consulting firm in Albuquerque, New Mexico. Prior to starting his company, Bill was a wildlife biologist for the New Mexico Department of Game and Fish where he worked to conserve Lesser Prairie-Chickens, fur-bearers, black bears, mountain lions, and bighorn sheep. He holds a PhD in Biology with an emphasis in Landscape Ecology from the University of New Mexico.